MY TEAR BOTTLE

Janice —
Know Him &
Know your freeedom!

In Christ Alone —
Katie Faith
7-08

KATIE FAITH

MY TEAR
BOTTLE

A Poetic Journey

Pleasant Word
A Division of WINEPRESS PUBLISHING

Pleasant Word (a division of WinePress Publishing, PO Box 428, Enumclaw, WA 98022) functions only as book publisher. As such, the ultimate design, content, editorial accuracy, and views expressed or implied in this work are those of the author.

Unless otherwise noted, all Scriptures are taken from the *Holy Bible, New International Version*®, *NIV*®. Copyright © 1973, 1978, 1984 by the International Bible Society. Used by permission of Zondervan. All rights reserved.

ISBN 13: 978-1-4141-1105-6
ISBN 10: 1-4141-1105-3
Library of Congress Catalog Card Number: 2007906782

To the mighty infilling Holy Spirit,
without whom not one poem could
have been penned.

and

To Denise, you have been my "Jonathan."
1 Samuel 18:4

CONTENTS

AUTHOR'S NOTE

Therefore I am now going to allure her; I will lead her into the desert and speak tenderly to her. There I will give her back her vineyards and will make the Valley of Achor (trouble) a door of hope. There she will sing as in the days of her youth, as in the day she came up out of Egypt.

—Hosea. 2:14-15

I came to the beautiful Bitterroot Valley of Montana on the heels of a shattered relationship. Broken, hurting, and shamed, I began a journey of the soul. This valley is lined to the west by the Bitterroot Mountains and to the east by the Sapphires, truly one of the prettiest places in America. In the quiet, slow pace of this unusual countryside, God began to show me a picture of my heart and life up to that point. I heard Him speak tenderly within, *"Katie, as with these massive mountains to the west My child, you have a root of bitterness. Yet I am asking you to look east and take note of the Sapphires, which are filled with gems. I alone will carry you through this valley in your life, and you will come out from this bitterness of heart to shine as a sapphire within My hand."* Over the past three years I have been the recipient of God's much needed discipline and His amazing grace. In this time of much solitude, tears, and intercession, have come the poetry you have in your hand. It is my prayer that you are moved by the Spirit of God as you read what He alone has given me, and that as you meditate upon the words you will know Jesus to be full of grace and so very alive! We were created to bear His glory! Search the world over, yet never will you know a love like that which Christ offers.

...And by him we cry "Abba, Father." The Spirit himself testifies with our spirit that we are God's children.

—Romans 8:15-16

LITTLE GIRL

Little girl broken
By life's awful use
Looking for love
Finding only abuse

Lonely life
Hurting heart
Waves of sorrow
So much strife

Shattered dreams
Take time to heal
Tears like streams
Life's years reveal

Healing will come
By God's tender hand
His poured-out heart
On this plowed-up land

Blood runs down
Covering the ground
Where choices were wrong
My sins had me bound

His hands reach out
Holding this heart
Jagged and shattered
Life's torn it apart

Holding it high
He breathes His own life
My Daddy is found
She says with a sigh….

February 2005

…But I the Lord will answer them; I, the God of Israel, will not forsake them. I will make rivers flow on barren heights, and springs within the valleys…

—Isaiah. 41:17-18

BITTERROOT VALLEY

Oh Bitterroot Valley
Where dryness abounds
Your broken-hearted women
Kneel to the ground

We come hurting and thirsty
Seeking Your face
Pour out springs of Living Water
In this unholy place

So needy and wanting
Desiring Your grace
Where bitterness has grown
Let sapphires be known

Broken and shattered
By life's awful pain
Polish, renew us
Your Spirit regained

Rivers in this Valley
Springs that flow
Be the Jesus in Your children
That all Valley people know

April 2005

It is for freedom that Christ has set us free. Stand firm, then, and do not let yourselves be burdened again by a yoke of slavery.

—**Galatians 5:1**

BELIEVING GOD

I have been loosed
I've been set free
The chains of my past
Have fallen from me

Chains of abuse
Sorrow and shame
No longer have victory
No more am I lame

Believing God
Can do all things
I am who He says
A child of the King

Arrows of lies
Once shot through this heart
God's Word now my shield
Blocking each fiery dart

I am not what you say
Not bound by my past
He bore that for me
And I am set free!

April 2005

My sheep listen to my voice; I know them, and they follow me.

—John 10:27

LISTEN MY CHILD

Listen My child
Hear with your heart
My words are a lamp
From them do not depart

My lips to your ears
Speaking guidance and love
Don't say you can't hear
My angels above

I walk with you daily
I'm holding your hand
Just say that you need me
Before you I stand

I'm lifting your gaze
To look into Mine
Don't take your eyes from
  me
I'm yours for all time

There's love here for you
My heart's open wide
Don't look any further
I'm your place to hide

I'm Jesus the Son
God's Only One
And you are My child
For you I am wild!

June 2005

Cleanse me with hyssop, and I will be clean; wash me, and I will be whiter than snow.

—Psalm 51:7

WASH ME

Wash me in rivers
That make me clean
Wash me in rivers
Where You have been

Fill my mind
With all that You say
Walk with me, talk with me
Take me Your way

Shape my heart
By the power of Your hand
Willing and ready
At Your slightest command

May my lips
Be given to praise
Hands that worship
At Your name they raise

Holiness, Holiness
In all that I do
A life of worship
Given to you

July 2005

The mountains will bring prosperity to the people,
the hills the fruit of righteousness.

—Psalm 72:3

BIG SKIES

Oh Bitterroot Mountains
Covered in green
Majesty beauty
Like none I have seen

This valley below
Where I've come to dwell
God's hand here to hold me
In Him I am well

Sapphires of treasure
Lay to the east
Rolling and smooth
Like visions of peace

Here in this valley
Where rivers run wide
His love never leaves me
I'm held at His side

Big skies above
I'm nestled in grace
My Father has brought me
To this plentiful place!

August 2005

Charm is deceptive, and beauty is fleeting; but a woman who fears the Lord is to be praised.
—Proverbs 31:30

OH RIGHTEOUS WOMAN

The prayers of a righteous
   woman
Will reach My throne
My heart will be turned
To her alone

When My women kneel
And humbly bow down
The heavens unfold
And answers are found

Like Ruth or Naomi
Or Esther the Queen
When women are praying
My glory is seen!

Her face bent toward
   Heaven
Her tears I will dry
When My women pray
The angels reply

Don't store up your worries
Don't hold it all in
I'm moving upon you
Let freedom begin

Stay close to Me child
In word thought and prayer
Your lamps filled with oil
Righteous women are rare

October 2005

For I am convinced that neither death nor life, neither angels nor demons, neither the present nor the future, nor any powers, neither height nor depth, nor anything else in all creation, will be able to separate us from the love of God that is in Christ Jesus our Lord.

—Romans 8:38-39

TOO FAR

Did you fall again My
  darling?
Have you sinned beyond
  My blood?
That's what He'd like to tell
  you
Yet I am here in love

Has your heart been badly
  broken?
Are your tears too much to
  bear?
This life no bed of roses
I see and I've been there

You think you're no more
  useful
My grace won't go that far
He lies to you with pleasure
Your mind he strives to mar

Now let Me tell you
  sweetheart
He has no claim to you
I've all the scars to prove it
My love for you is true

Stop listening to deception
Look up My precious bride
I've crushed his head
  beneath Me
I've drawn you to My side

Come lie here in My
  chambers
My breath upon your face
I've plans for you beloved
My heart your resting place

October 2005

"When Satan reminds you of your past, remind him of his future."

—author unknown

You will again have compassion on us; you will tread our sins underfoot and hurl our iniquities into the depths of the sea.

—Micah 7:19

PRODIGAL CHILD

I'm right here
Can't look back there
The past is now past
This burden He'll bear

So many poor choices
Seasons of sin
I can't make it right
In flesh we don't win

Can't beat myself up nor
  wallow in pity
Those I have hurt…those
  who've hurt me
Covered in the blood
Buried in the sea

I've mulled it all over
Cried hundreds of tears
I've run from you Lord
Hiding in fear

What the enemy stole
With all of his lies
You've waited to claim
Your Prodigal Child

Your love never left
In my wandering pain
Looking from Heaven
Your lamb to regain

When will I get it, Will I
  ever learn?
You're Abba the Father,
  Jesus His Son
You love me each moment
As Your only one

October 2005

For my precious sister in Christ, *Stevie*. It is my prayer that as you hold this book in your hands, you will now be the recipient of a healthy and perfectly matched kidney. You, dear one, have been an outstanding example of Job-like endurance while exuding a joy that could only come from a Spirit-filled heart! I love you girlfriend! *I always thank my God as I remember you in my prayers.* (Philemon 4)

For he will command his angels concerning you to guard you in all your ways...

—Psalm 91:11

SWEET DREAMS

Lie with me Lord
As a husband would do
Capture my dreams
All glory for You

Come to this bed
Where I lay my head
Whisper Your way
Til morrows new day

Your breath on my neck
Your hand to my brow
My mind given over
My King speaks His vow

I'll keep you He says
Don't worry My love
My angels surround you
From Heaven above

They're here in this room
Their shields lifted high
All singing sweet dreams
No more will he lie

So sleep precious child
My arms around you
No waking in fear
Jehovah is here

October 2005

When she poured out this perfume on my body, she did it to prepare me for burial. I tell you the truth, wherever this gospel is preached throughout the world, what she has done will also be told in memory of her.

—Matthew 26:12-13

ALABASTER WOMAN

Oh Alabaster Woman
As with the box you bear
Your heart has so been
  broken
Your life does show the
  wear

Drawn to the Master
While others condemn
Bowing behind Him
His precious gem

Breaking the box
Your most precious gift
The oil poured out
Your sin He did lift

Unworthy they say
A woman of shame
Yet He reaches out
Your heart to reclaim

Your tears like a river
To His feet they flow
You worship the Savior
That others would know

He touched your dark
  places
He lifted your head
This Jesus you bow to
His heart now your bed

No more condemnation
The past is now past
And this changing moment
Is all that will last

October 2005

The sacrifices of God are a broken spirit; a broken and contrite heart, O God, you will not despise.
—Psalm 51:17

SURRENDER

All expectation falling away
All my dreams kept at bay
Your will and hand leading
  me now
To Your loving plan my
  knee must bow

Tried for years going my
  way
Looking for love and hope
  in man
Now laid at your altar
My heart in Your hand

My eyes raised to Heaven
My ears to Your voice
Whatever the path
Will now be Your choice

I'll bow in this life
At Your nail-pierced feet
I'll seek Your direction
Lord make me complete

I'm not what I was
Yet not what I'll be
My hand to the plow
You're working in me

My life given over
As clay in Your hand
Use me for glory
Your will my command

Don't spare what is needed
Fill this broken cup
I'll look to no other
While You fill me up

October 2005

To every sister who has ever crossed my path and been kind enough to give a word of *reproof, grace,* or *love.* I have grown and been sharpened because of each of you!

> *As iron sharpens iron, so one man sharpens another.*
>
> —Proverbs 27:17

SWEET LAMBS

Women of God
Sent from His heart
Like arrows of love
All playing their part

My sisters bring strength
To gird up this soul
As beacons of light
Accepting their role

His hand sends them to me
This journey to share
A garden of flowers
With beauty so rare

I look to the Father
Yet listen in love
As He works through
   women
Like rain from above

You need one another
He whispers to me
My women as iron
Pour strength into thee

I love you my sisters
In Him we are one
Sweet Lambs of the Father
Through Jesus the Son

November 2005

For Kristi—May He bless all that you put your heart and mind to!

God is within her, she will not fall; God will help her at break of day.

—Psalm 46:5

GLORY IN YOU

My little girl
That's who you are
I walked with you child
In that schoolyard

You weren't alone
Bearing all their attacks
The wounds you received
Were *all* on My back

As your heart bore pain
Your Abba stood close
Where Satan did sift
I grew your gift

Others have hurt you
So you'd know the pain
Now older and wiser
My lambs we will claim

Don't stay in this shame
There's work we must do
My precious child
I see glory in you

Step out of this sorrow
Where he has you bound
I've bright new tomorrows
The lost must be found

November 2006

These words came out of an overwhelming concern for the lost. I pray that everyone would know Jesus and experience the wild romance He alone offers!

My lover spoke and said to me, "Arise, my darling, my beautiful one, and come with me.
—Song of Songs 2:10

YOUR PRINCE

I'm here in this room
My Spirit is falling
And this dance is yours
It's your name I'm calling

Before you I'm standing
For your hand I reach
Arise in this moment
Your heart I will teach

Your Prince in white robes
Has stepped from his
   throne
I've sought you for ages
To make you My own

Don't tarry My darling
Don't stay in your seat
I've secrets to tell you
Of life that's complete

I've come just for you
Your heart I must claim
Not leaving this room
Til you know My Name

I'm Jesus the Lamb
The Truth and The Way
My name is I AM
Jehovah Yahweh!

November 2005

Love the Lord your God with all your heart and with all your soul and with all your strength.
—**Deuteronomy 6:5**

ALL OF ME

Lord fill my mind
With thoughts of You
Clarity, Vision
For all that is true

Focus my eyes
On Your face alone
Holding my gaze
Your heart will be known

Impart unto me
Ears that will hear
The voice of my Master
Ever so clear

The coal to my lips
That Your love would flow
Cleanse each passing word
Your seeds I would sow

My heart as Your own
Where Your angels sing
All holiness dwells
A place for my King

Use these hands
That they would reach out
Lord plant my feet
Where there is no doubt

My spirit for truth
Anoint me I pray
Now I can go forth
To face each new day

November 2005

Of all the women in the Bible, I relate the most to this woman. Her longings, her shame, her thirst, and at long last, her *joy* as she meets the Master and finally draws from the right well!

Everyone who drinks this water will be thirsty again, but whoever drinks the water I give him will never thirst. Indeed the water I give him will become in him a spring of water welling up to eternal life.

—John 4:13-14

WOMAN OF THIRST

Alone and in shame
She comes to the well
Thirsting for something
Her heart cannot tell

Waiting to greet her
The Master is there
Asking for water
His love He will share

But I am a sinner
And You are a King
How can this be?
You make my heart sing

My bed has known many
My feet walk in shame
Yet You are the water
My thirst You will claim

My coming, My going
You've known every one
Seeing right through me
My heart is undone

You must be salvation
The Christ spoken of
I cannot deny it
This heavenly love

Oh Jesus the Master
The well I draw from
This woman knows healing
Now that You've come

November 2005

Be sure to fear the Lord and serve him faithfully with all your heart; consider what great things he has done for you.

—1 Samuel 12:24

CONSIDER ME

Consider Me child
Consider My love
Dwell on My word
On all that I've done

In all your big plans
For this year to come
Take hold of My hand
Reach out to someone

You've goals and high hopes
Of all that you'll do
Do they include Me?
May I come with you?

The changes you'll make
The things that you dream
Have you sought My will?
Are you on My team?

This year could be rich
Your gifts could unfold
If what you chase after
Is heavenly gold

This world holds
   temptation
And ladders to climb
Oh be given over
Remember you're Mine

Consider My life
Consider the blood
Consider a year
My glory could flood

December 2005
(New Years Eve)

*Listen O daughter, consider and give ear: Forget
your people and your father's house. The king is
enthralled by your beauty; honor him for he is
your lord.*

—Psalm 45:10-11

YOUR ESTHER

I am Your Esther
You are my King
You've bathed me in love
My heart does now sing

The journey's been long
As stumbling I've come
Your hand ever strong
My love You have won

My Pillar My Rock
My Light in the night
When all others fled
Your angels did fight

My soul You have captured
My heart now Your home
My value established
I kneel at Your throne

I'll stand as Your queen
Your robes cover me
On You I will lean
In glory I'm free

You've made my life pure
My past washed away
All joy now restored
On this brand new day

Oh Jesus my Lord
Salvation and Sword
Your handmaiden bows
For You are adored

December 2005

Come to me, all you who are weary and burdened and I will give you rest.

—Matthew 11:28

DANCING BEFORE YOU

What hurts you My child?
What sorrow so great?
What burden too heavy?
I'll carry that weight

I'm right here with you
I'll stand at your side
Your sadness My burden
In Me you can hide

Your face holds such pain
Your heart so downcast
I'm drawing you closer
Away from your past

There's nothing so awful
No place that's so dark
My blood covered all this
Your life is My mark

I'm reaching to hold you
To love and forgive
There's dancing before you
A life you must live

Don't stay in your sadness
Don't carry regret
Your Abba, Your Daddy
Will help you forget

Like oil to your sorrow
I'm poured out for you
I love you oh dear one
Step into My truth

December 2005

As obedient children, do not conform to the evil desires you had when you lived in ignorance, but just as he who called you is holy, so be holy in all you do...

—1 Peter 1:14-15

YUCKY SOMETIMES

I'm yucky sometimes
Not Christ-like at all
I'm human so often
Not standing so tall

My flesh hinders me
My ugliness roars
I push Him aside
Where I could have soared

My words aren't so kind
Where they could have
  been
Forgetting my Lord
My focus on men

He waits in the wings
My spirit to calm
Forgiveness He brings
His love like a balm

I keep falling down
He kneels helping me
A pauper A King
He's setting me free

I see you through love
He says with a smile
This work to be done
Will take us awhile

This temple you dwell in
Will soon reflect Me
For I am the builder
My glory you'll see

January 2006

But seek first his kingdom and his righteousness, and all these things will be given to you as well.
—Matthew 6:33

LET GO

Let go My child
Don't hang onto that
Don't worry Don't fret
You know where I'm at

Get into My word
Oh drink from the well
Lay everything down
I'll listen, you tell

Turn over each worry
Don't start this new day
Before you give over
And walk in My way

Let go of your loved ones
Give all that to Me
Now focus your heart child
It's Me you must see

Like baggage so heavy
Set all of it down
Not yours to be carried
Your heart can't be bound

This day holds such treasure
I've blessings for you
Don't miss it My darling
I'm making things new

No worries No burdens
Leave all that behind
Look up to your Daddy
My joy you will find

January 2006

Each of us should please his neighbor for his good, to build him up.

—Romans 15:1-2

SURROUNDED BY FLOWERS

I sit right beside you
Yet I know you not
I see that you're hurting
Such pain you have fought

A secret I'll tell you
I've sat where you are
So broken and fearful
Yet I've come so far

These women around you
Hold treasure so deep
Let your heart be open
Such healing you'll reap

No secret so awful
No pain you have known
Is more than your sisters'
His love will be shown

This study you've come to
A safe place to dwell
Surrounded by flowers
Your heart will get well

We mean you no harm here
Our hearts know your pain
So rest in God's love dear
There's much to be gained

When this time is over
We'll smile as we greet
His hand knits our hearts
Each time that we meet

You don't know this woman
Who sits next to you
Yet God just may use her
To make your heart new

January 2006

For you created my inmost being, you knit me together in my mother's womb. I praise you because I am fearfully and wonderfully made; your works are wonderful, I know that full well.

—Psalm 139:13-14

PRICELESS

You're valuable to me
You're priceless can't you see
I've shed My blood for you
Now walk as if you're free

Don't hang your head so
  low
Don't buy into his lies
Your worth is found in Me
It's mirrored in My eyes

I hung upon the cross
I laid there in that grave
That you would know true
  life
It's you I came to save

The hairs upon your head
I know them one by one
Before you took one breath
I made the morning sun

I am your Daddy, child
I formed you in the womb
My life is in your veins
For you there'll be no tomb

I know your every thought
You're written on My heart
In all your falling down
I've loved you from the start

Each day as you awake
My heart does wait for you
Let My love fill the place
You've thought there was no
  grace

January 2006

Be self-controlled and alert. Your enemy the devil prowls around like a roaring lion looking for someone to devour. Resist him, standing firm in the faith.

—1 Peter 5:8-9

STAND FIRM

There's battle before you
Now shod up your feet
Your enemy prowls
With him you will meet

Pick up your sword
The Word of the Lord
Prepare for this fight
As you stand in God's light

Belted by truth
His lies cannot pierce
Stand firm on the Rock
His tactics are fierce

All righteousness covers
The heart of My child
The tempter will come
Do not be defiled

Now hold tight your shield
Great faith you must wield
Your enemy lurks
To bring down My work

Stand firm I have said
Don't give up your ground
The sword of My Spirit
Will soon have him bound

And now My salvation
Will cover your head
This battle was won
When My blood was shed

January 2006

At some point in everyone's life, we each must answer the question: *"Who do you say that He is?"* Pondering this in my own heart, these words came from what I know my God to be.

Trust in the Lord forever, for the Lord, the Lord, is the Rock eternal.

—Isaiah 26:4

NO OTHER

Where I stood shaking
You firm me up
When my world crumbles
You fill my cup

Where my enemy lurks
Your angels do trod
When my heart fails
You alone are my God

The praise of my lips
Will rise to You
My one request
Lord make me new

No other god
Ever has stood
Amongst a people
Bearing so much good

Light to all darkness
Healing and Life
Holy and Priceless
You've made me Your wife

Who is this God
Who runs after me?
Only one motive
That I would be free

You're Jesus—Jehovah
With arms open wide
My Husband and Savior
Oh come take Your Bride!

January 2006

But he was pierced for our transgressions, he was crushed for our iniquities; and the punishment that brought us peace was upon him, by his wounds we are healed.

—Isaiah 53:5

THE SACRIFICE

Seven times Your blood
Was poured out for me
Each time to the Father
You bent Your knee

At the Mount of Olives
You bowed to pray
Blood fell to the ground
You will be the way

Mocked and beaten
They struck Your face
Wounding my Savior
You're taking my place

Barabbas set free
Now flogged for Your love
Your own cannot see
Their Father above

Stripped then robed
They spat upon You
A crown of thorns
Hail King of the Jews

Hands that brought life
Now nailed to a tree
A Lamb led to slaughter
That all could be free

Now look to the One
We all did pierce
The water the blood
A love that is fierce

He died just for you
We have heard it said
Believe it my friend
He rose from the dead

The way has been paved
Don't turn left or right
Christ's blood has been shed
On earth's darkest night

Oh once a slain Lamb
His blood running down
Now King of my heart
To Him I am bound

February 2006

"In that day," declares the Lord, *you will call me 'my husband'; you will no longer call me 'my master.'*

—Hosea 2:16

MY VALENTINE

Heart of all hearts
God among men
Love everlasting
Cleansing from sin

My Valentine
Husband to me
Love like no other
Your face I will see

Hands that reach down
Heart open wide
Forgiveness flows free
You stand at my side

Song of Songs
That's who You are
Cupid's arrow
Shot from afar

Straight to my heart
You've aimed Your love
I'll not know another
Sweet Spirit and Dove

Oh Jesus my healing
Your grace changes all
I've fallen for You Lord
My life heeds Your call

I Love You, I Love You
Can You hear my heart?
I marry You Jesus
For You set apart

February 2006

...As a bridegroom rejoices over his bride, so will your God rejoice over you.

—Isaiah 62:5

SWEET FAIR LADY

I'm calling you to freedom
My arms are open wide
I've waited for you darling
Come stand here at My side

You've listened long enough
To all of Satan's lies
Come nestle in My arms
I've heard your every cry

Don't tarry any longer
He means you only harm
Yet I have sent My angels
You need not be alarmed

Where he has meant to
    wound
My body bore your pain
Now I am here to clothe
    you
In heavenly healing rain

Step out of all the darkness
Stand firm within My light
I've come for you alone
    child
You're precious in My sight

Let all your tears flow freely
Let all defenses down
I'm standing right before
    you
I have your wedding gown

You are My bride dear
    woman
I'm Christ your coming
    King
I've named you Sweet Fair
    Lady
Today your heart will sing

February 2006

I am the Alpha and the Omega, the First and the Last, the Beginning and the End.

—Revelation 22:13

GARDEN TO GRAVE

A garden so perfect
Where Adam walked free
Only one choice
Don't eat of this tree

Satan stepped in
Tempting their souls
Eve bends her ear
Now sin takes its toll

God must intervene
Where death would have
  its way
Now guarding Eden's door
For choices… you will pay

Yet He is not a God
Who leaves us on our own
He'll pave another way
His Son must die alone

Only one life
Can cover the cost
The blood of God's Lamb
Redeeming the lost

It is finished… Christ has
  said
I will rise from the dead
He may have bruised your
  heel
Yet I will crush his head

From the garden to the
  grave
Christ turned it all around
His blood has done the
  work
Eve's tempter will be bound

February 2006

I am the way and the truth and the life. No one comes to the Father except through me.

—John 14:6

NO MORE LIES

She's lookin' at me
She must think I'm fat
I shouldn't have come
I feel like a rat

She doesn't like me
She's prettier too
She has it together
Now I'm feelin' blue

Should have stayed home
I don't belong here
They all have such gifts
I'll sit in the rear

They smile like they care
But I know the truth
I'll never fit in
I'm nobody's Ruth

They have nicer clothes
They drive nicer cars
Could I be like them
They shine like such stars

But what's that I hear
The voice of the King
He's speaking to me
His truth He will bring

You've listened to lies
These women love you
Afraid like you are
They have their wounds too

Don't listen to voices
That tear you apart
I'm Jesus your truth
I'm healing your heart

February 2006

Five-year-old Faith stood in front of me twirling in her pretty Sunday dress as I asked, "How are you, sweetheart?" She replied with these words. "Katie, did you know that the angels are waiting for us to come out and play?" When asked how she knew this, she replied that God had told her and that He talks to her all the time!

Jesus said, "Let the little children come to me, and do not hinder them, for the kingdom of heaven belongs to such as these.
—Matthew 19:14

COME OUT AND PLAY

My angels are waiting
Oh come out and play
I made you for joy
From nothing but clay

Oh, Precious Faith
You hear My voice
It's good you're so little
You drown out the noise

You know who I Am
You hear when I speak
When no one is looking
We play Hide-n-Seek

It's nothing for you
To skip, dance, and twirl
We laugh all the time
Cause you are My girl

Big people get crazy
Go through life so fast
Yet you know the secret
I'm all that will last

You come take my hands
We spin all around
And lean back our heads
Let laughter abound

I'm Jesus Sweet Faith
I love you it's true
Don't grow up too fast
We've dancing to do

When you do get big
Oh please don't forget
The fun that we had
And how that we met

Take with you My child
This little girl's heart
Stay so close to Me
With each day's new start

Before we can blink
You'll grow to a lady
But never forget
That you are My baby

February 2006,
for Faith Thayer

Burst into songs of joy together, you ruins of Jerusalem, for the Lord has comforted His people, He has redeemed Jerusalem.

—Isaiah 52:9

HER HEART IN MY CHEST

Who was this woman
After that day
A prostitute with perfume
Is all they could say

Yet she knew different
Bathed in His love
No longer the harlot
Now touched by the Dove

As she arose
In leaving that room
Accepting forgiveness
She'd met with her Groom

I know her too well
Her heart's in my chest
The depths of her sin
And finding no rest

The one with the spikenard
Known all over town
Is now the King's bride
In her wedding gown

The void won't be filled
Is what she did learn
Til once and for all
To Jesus you turn

She'll not be forgotten
I'm sure when we meet
Together we'll sit
At our Savior's feet

March 2006

The Lord will march out like a mighty man, like a warrior he will stir up his zeal; with a shout he will raise the battle cry and will triumph over his enemies.

—Isaiah 42:13

MARCH FORTH

Adam marched out
From the garden that day
Eve at his side
Not knowing their way

Abraham marched
With Isaac in tow
Some fire, some wood
His faith he did show

The Jews led by Moses
Marched to their promised
   land
Grumbling and stumbling
Yet by God's mighty hand

Marching 'round Jericho
Trumpets did blast
Joshua obeyed
All that God asked

Marching through life
Leaving us Psalms
David wrote words
As God's healing balm

Esther marched forward
To honor a king
Oh God spare my people
Your praises we'll sing

Job marched on
Through illness and pain

I'll believe in my God
Even though I am slain

A march for the lost
The apostles went out
Commanded by Jesus
Removing all doubt

Timothy, Titus
And Paul marching through
Recording God's Word
That we might know too

You've read all God's tales
Of marching for Him
Warriors for glory
When things seemed so dim

Many years passed
Yet all still holds true
No different from them
We've marching to do

His saints gone before us
Are counting on me
To march for my Jesus
That others might see

March 2006
for Sue
(March 4th is the only day of
   the year with a command.)

And why do you worry about clothes? See how the lilies of the field grow. They do not labor or spin. Yet I tell you that not even Solomon in all his splendor was dressed like one of these.
—Matthew 6:28-29

CONSIDER THE LILIES

Consider how the lilies
  grow
They do not labor or spin
Consider how your heart
  would grow
If Christ could dwell
  therein

Consider how your days
  would go
Inviting the Lord along
Consider years of walking
  with Him
A woman in Christ is
  strong

What if the path you
  choose to take
Includes some prayer each
  day
Opening up your heart dear
  one
Asking Him to stay

Consider laying down your
  strife
A mind that wrestles with
  worry
Consider putting Jesus first
Lay down un-needed hurry

As with the lilies that grow
  in beauty
They reach as for the sun
God's Son could be our
  reaching too
Each day to Him we run

Lilies filled with sweet
  perfume
As women filled to brim
Aroma of our precious Lord
As oil that pours from Him

So be as beauty of God's
  field
Stand tall and worry not
He cares for lilies
  everywhere
Your life His heart has
  sought

Oh precious lilies thirst no
  more
Your Living Water has come
Jesus the Lamb is raining
  down
The Savior God's Chosen
  One!

March 2006

His head and hair were white like wool, as white as snow, and his eyes were like blazing fire. His feet were like bronze glowing in a furnace, and his voice was like the sound of rushing waters.
—**Revelation 1:14-15**

THE LION IS ROARING

The Lion of Judah
Is sleeping no more
The Lion of Judah
Has begun to roar

The Heavens are quaking
With undue rest
The Lion is pacing
I see fire in His chest

This Lion of Moses
On Mount Sinai did burn
Now coming for His
  children
Is planning His return

The Lion who laid Pharaoh
  low
Is pawing Heaven's ground
A roar of holy righteousness
Will soon melt idols down

He's not the stricken Lamb
  you knew
He will not hang His head
This time His eyes ablaze
  with fire
He'll judge all living and
  dead

Warrior and King, My
  Mighty God
With hair as white as snow
Feet as bronze held to the
  fire
His face a brilliant glow

All Heaven will rumble
His angels await
The word of their King
Now open the gates

All glory comes forth
On stallions of white
Hells keys in His hand
Earth's battle He'll fight

My Alpha, Omega
Morning Star and Groom
Lord of all Lords
Defeating the tomb

Be ready God's chosen
Your robes dipped in blood
The sound of His roar
Comes in like a flood!

March 2006

...Bring my sons from afar and my daughters from the ends of the earth—everyone who is called by my name, whom I created for my glory, whom I formed and made.

—Isaiah 43:6-7

HOUSE OF GLORY

A house for Your glory
That's what I want to be
A place for God's story
That everyone might see

Shining just like Jesus
Bright as God's own Son
A life that makes them
  notice
A heart that Christ has won

I wanna shine for You Lord
I wanna show Your love
I wanna be so different
That we are hand in glove

A temple where you dwell
  Lord
A place of holiness
Your Spirit flowing freely
Your hand upon me rests

Not bound by earthly
  trappings
Not seeking worldly toys
Walking in Your footsteps
A child of Daddy's joy

It's not enough to live here
To go to work each day
Just trodding through this
  life
Seeking my own way

I've got to serve the Savior
My life must be His throne
I cannot find my breath
  Lord
Outside of You alone

A house for Jesus' glory
Where His robes fill the
  room
Not just any woman
One living for her Groom

March 2006

73

The Lord has made proclamation to the ends of the earth: say to the Daughter of Zion, 'See your Savior comes!'

—Isaiah 62:11

LITTLE JEWISH GIRL

Little Jewish girl
Precious chosen one
Jehovah smiling down on
  you
That you might know His
  Son

As Mary of Nazareth
With kindness in your eyes
I'm reminded of her
In the way that you shine

My heart in wonder
As I stood before you
Does she know my Jesus,
That He came for her too?

Marcey, House of God
He knit you in the womb
And for this very day
He's risen from the tomb

Pick up your Bible child
Learn what Prophets told
Your King would walk this
  earth
The truth for you unfolds

Now listen to your heart
Where lies a still small voice
You'll recognize it soon
There'll be no other choice

My heart goes out to you
God meant for us to meet
I've Jewish blood too
I bow at Jesus' feet

Jesus looks for you
His eyes can't leave your
  face
He's asking for your hand
He'll be your resting place

The God of Abraham
The line that you come
  from
Written in Christ's hands
Precious chosen one

March 2006

May he strengthen your hearts so that you will be blameless and holy in the presence of our God and Father when our Lord Jesus comes with all his holy ones.

—1 Thessalonians 3:13

MORE

I want Your heart Lord
Yours beating in mine
I want Your heart Lord
My spirit refined

Give me Your sight Lord
Eyes that see through
To where there is hurt Lord
I'll offer Your truth

I want the mind of Christ
A wisdom from above
I want to think Your
thoughts
Discernment with pure love

You speak the truth in love
Your lips waste not one
word
Could my speech reflect
Yours
A tongue that You would
gird

Attentively listening
To all of our cries
Attune my ears Lord
To Your children's sighs

More of You Jesus
Is my heart's desire
Plant Your Spirit in me
To burn with great fire

April 2006

I baptize you with water for repentance. But after me will come one who is more powerful than I, whose sandals I am not fit to carry. He will baptize you with the Holy Spirit and with fire.
—Matthew 3:11

FORM WITH POWER

This form where I dwell
Must have power from on
   high
Not just steeped in mere
   tradition
No, on eagles wings I fly!

Not do this and Oh do that
Not man's rule upon mere
   rule
I'm talkin' Holy Spirit-filled
With fire of heavenly fuel!

I can't just read the Word
   each day
I must eat what God has
   said
My spirit craving every
   word
Old man risen from the
   dead!

Not just singing pretty
   words
From hymnal page to page
Now God's songbird, I'm
   set free
From man's traditional cage

Sit down stand up
Now repeat after me
Can't follow that crowd
I'm walkin' on God's sea!

I'll enter the building
On Sunday to meet
But, I am the temple
I've God's fire in my feet!

As David danced in
Bringing God's ark
Don't ask me to sit
Praising Christ is my mark!

Too long God's people
Have been form without
   power
Baptize us in fire
Let this be the hour!

May 2006
for Jim and Clare

In the last days, God says, I will pour out My Spirit on all people...

—Acts 2:17

WOMAN ABLAZE

Put Your laws in my mind
Write Your word on my
  heart
Be Lord in this woman
Bound to You set apart

Use me for Your glory
My eyes set on You
Your ways become mine
As I walk in Your truth

Speak boldly through me
A tongue of holy fire
Honed by the Father
Seeking only His desire

A woman ablaze
The prophetic poured out
A walkin' talkin' vessel
I teach Jesus, You slay doubt

Burn away all dross
Mold me by Your hand
Send me to the lost
In righteousness I'll stand

Heal the broken-hearted
Everywhere we teach
Breathe life into me Jesus
The multitudes we'll reach

Breathe faithfulness on me
Sold out to You alone
Found bowed before my
  King
Prostrate before Your throne

Use me in this life
Oh Lord wipe clean my
  past
Covered in Your robes
What's lived for You will
  last

I'm new I'm new
In love with You
I run this race
To see God's face

May 2006

How can you say to your brother, 'Let me take the speck out of your eye,' when all the time there is a plank in your own eye?

—Matthew 7:4

SHOW LOVE

I'm all about mercy
I'm all about love
You can't meet the law
So I've sent the Dove

Don't beat yourself up
With rule upon rule
Stand in My freedom
I'll make you My jewel

Don't look at others
Judging their lives
Keep eyes on your Father
Step out of all strife

I'll take care of that one
While I'm honing you
Keep eyes on your Abba
I'll show them what's true

You can't fix a brother
With that log in your eye
Show grace to each other
I'll teach them to fly

I've so much to change
Within you Dear One
Stop solving their problem
We've work to get done

I've called you to love
To speak of My worth
Stop looking around
Stand kind in new birth

Don't trod on My grace
By walking in sin
Be led by My Spirit
Stop looking at men

Show love to your brother
Tend your house My friend
My grace must flow from
   you
I've your knees to bend!

May 2006

Go into all the world and preach the good news to all creation. Whoever believes and is baptized will be saved, but whoever does not believe will be condemned.

—Mark 16:15

RESURRECTION VALLEY

Resurrection Valley
Where My people come to
dwell
I've placed you here for
reason
Of Christ Jesus you might
tell

Walk boldly here My
children
Speak love where ere you go
Don't hide your lamp, Oh
dear one
There's seed that we must
sow

The broken here are many
There's healing to be done
I've come to walk beside
you
That hurting souls are won

Now don yourselves with
shield and sword
Prepare your feet with peace
Speak freely of Salvation's
Son
Those saved by grace
increase

This Bitterroot Valley
I've claimed for My own
Missoula to Sula
My love must be sown

Rid yourselves of poverty
thinking
Your Father is the King
No place for grumbling
Israelites
Go out with hearts that sing

This valley is MINE
I claim it as such
Get over yourselves
There are hearts we must
touch

July 2006

He cuts off every branch in me that bears no fruit,
while every branch that does bear fruit, he prunes
so that it will be even more fruitful.

— **John 15:2**

UNPLOWED GROUND

Unplowed ground
Where thorns have grown
Life's learned sin
Habits I've sown

I know I'm forgiven
I know I'm Your child
Yet gardens need pruning
Where weeds have grown
  wild

It's painful at times
To look deep inside
Accepting the shears
Dying to pride

I say I want more
More Jesus in me
Yet being like You Lord
Will take bended knees

I give You permission
To prune, shape, and mold
To do needed work
Refine me as gold

I'm made for my Father
Created to serve
From this holy calling
May I never swerve

July 2006

He has taken me to the banquet hall, and his banner over me is love.

—Song of Songs 2:4

ONLY ONE TABLE

Eat and run
That's what they say
And that's what we do
When from Jesus we stray

So much to choose from
In this world where we live
So many distractions
With nothing to give

We fill up our eyes
We tickle our ears
While pleasing our flesh
We're wasting the years

This world is a playground
Where we chase after toys
Men needing Jesus
Yet acting like boys

Filling our lives
With things that will burn
Dancing with the Devil
Will we ever learn

God waits in the wings
His heart oh so true!
From before you were born
He'd made plans for you

The things of this earth
Cannot satisfy
Oh come to His table
Where we'll never die

Only one table
Where we're meant to eat
God's laid it *all* out
At our Savior's feet

August 2006

I saw heaven standing open and there before me was a white horse, whose rider is called Faithful and True. With justice He judges and makes war.

—Revelation 19:11

HIS WHITE HORSE

He walked these hills of
   sunshine and green
His master's love could
   always be seen
A beautiful horse from
   God's own hand
Running to you at the
   slightest command

White horses are special
God's word tells me so
He'll ride one someday
His glory to show

They go home to Him, all
   one by one
Where pastures are greener
   and strength is renewed
The armies of Heaven need
   them you see
Returning one day to set us
   all free

The body you see
Where life seems no more
Has galloped to Heaven
On Christ's distant shore

Dear heart, be not troubled
God knows him by name
He's now at His side
With wind in his mane

As Christ comes to claim
His children one day
Your horse will be with
   Him
Leading the way

August 2006
For Dr. Bob & Pat,
Walk with God dear ones.

Behold, I am coming soon! My reward is with me,
and I will give to everyone according to what he
has done.

—**Revelation 22:12**

HOLY SCROLLS

The scrolls of life
Are in God's hand
His eyes raise up
In Heaven He stands

These Holy Scrolls
He's begun to close
Get ready My Son
For this You arose

The earth must pass away
All evil to an end
My children home to stay
My angels I will send

Not much time
Left for this Sodom
My grace reaches far
Yet these people have hit
  bottom

Sin abounds
Where I intended love
My heart can't take
What I see from above

This earth I created
Where men would fear God
Yet hearts have grown
  hardened
So far from My garden

Don't worry My children
This earth I'll destroy
My saints will come home
For you are My joy

Time is so short
Keep focused My child
My Son comes in glory
To finish this story

August 2006

Yours O Lord, is the greatness and the power and the glory and the majesty and the splendor, for everything in heaven and earth is yours. Yours, O Lord, is the kingdom; You are exalted as head over all.

—1 Chronicles 29:11

GOD MOST HIGH

Elohiym Adonai
Glory glory
God Most High

I worship You
I hold You dear
You are my Lord
I have no fear

God over all
Mountains bow down
My Abba my Daddy
The saints will resound

No other like You Lord
No one holds Your place
Righteous in judgment
Yet pouring out grace

Gentile and Jew
Will bow to Your name
Your Son soon returns
Revealing Your fame

Hands lifted high
Knees to the ground
ALL HAIL MY KING
Let praises abound!

September 2006

While they were eating, Jesus took bread, and gave thanks and broke it, and gave it to his disciples, saying, 'Take it; this is my body. Then he took the cup, gave thanks and offered it to them, and they all drank from it.

—Mark 14:22-23

CRACKERS AND JUICE

Some crackers and juice
Is that what we hold?
What could this mean?
A story's been told

Some bread and some wine
You hold here today
Don't miss the great cost
His blood paves the way

A long time ago
Christ carried His cross
Climbed one lonely hill
With hope for the lost

A crown and some thorns
A dark lonely hill
Not just a mere story
Forgiveness fulfilled

Beyond recognition
They beat Him dear one
Mocking then spitting
On God's Holy Son

Please don't take this lightly
Don't leave here today
Mocking the One
Who's shown you the way

He could have called angels
Thousands would heed
In silent submission
He knew our great need

Some crackers—some juice
That's not what we hold
His body—His blood
The TRUTH has been told

November 2006

For to us a child is born, to us a Son is given, and the government will be on His shoulders. And He will be called Wonderful Counselor, Mighty God, everlasting father, Prince of Peace.

—Isaiah 9:6

A SAVIOR NOT SANTA

A Savior not Santa
A manger and hay
Where cattle are lowing
No reindeer—no sleigh

No elves in green tights
No credit card debt
No hustle or bustle
Oh what shall I get?!

Ipods and diamonds
Cell phones and clothes
All things that are passing
In bright shiny bows

Santa's face is everywhere
Believe! Believe! they say
All hoping to receive a gift
In Mary's arms He lay

God's little baby boy
Born long ago in a stable
Holiness in swaddling
   clothes
Only to be called a fable

Joseph and Mary
Kiss His precious head
He'll save His people
The angel had said

A virgin—God's vessel
Wise men from afar
All for one baby
God's Bright Morning Star!

Oh nothing wrong with
   Santa
Make believe is fun
Don't miss the truth of
   Christmas
God's One and Only Son!

A Baby—My King
A Child—My Lord
A gift from the Father
My Savior adored!

December 2006
   Christmas Eve

God said to Moses, 'I AM who I AM.' This is what you are to say to the Israelites; I AM has sent me to you.

—Exodus 3:14

ONLY JESUS

Only my Lord
Could create this whole
  earth
Then stoop down to me
Imparting great worth

Only Jehovah
Could part the Red Sea
Wipe out Egyptians
Set Israelites free

Only Yeshua
Made Joshua stand tall
Pouring out strength
He brought down that wall

Only Jesus
Turned water to wine
Displaying His power
Before it was time

Only God's Son
Could fast day and night
Look Satan in the eye
YOU'LL NOT WIN THIS
  FIGHT!

Only the Master
Would wait at the well
All for one woman
Her thirst He would quell

Only one Lamb
Would be led up that hill
Freely lay down His life
For His Father's will

Only Jesus
Has done *all* these things
Returning one day
He'll ride angels' wings

Only my Lord
Could love me this much
Know all of my sorrow
And heal with His touch

Yes! Only the Christ
Is reaching for you
Oh serve Me dear one
Now what will you do?

January 2007

Therefore keep watch, because you do not know the day or the hour.

—Matthew 25:13

I'M WAITING MY LOVE

I'm eagerly waiting
I'm watching for You
My lamp filled with oil
My heart tried now true

As watchmen do wait
From walls dark by night
Armed by Your Spirit
Oh King be my might

Your word is the oil
Filling my soul
Your woman this lamp
Your glory my goal

I don't know the day
One can't know the hour
Yet I must be ready
When You come in power

A thief in the night
My heart You prepare
A wedding awaits
A love oh so rare

You're coming for me
You'll step from the throne
I'm waiting My Love
Oh come take me home

December 2006

Woe to you, teachers of the law and Pharisees, you hypocrites! You are like whitewashed tombs, which look beautiful on the outside but on the inside are full of dead men's bones and everything unclean.

—Matthew 23:27

CLEAN SHINY CHURCHES

Clean shiny churches
With bright white walls
Lives for appearance
Pride comes before the fall

Stained glass windows
Candles burning bright
Don't we look holy?
Forgetting God's true Light

Religious law givers
Pharisees He said
Blinded by law
Walking talking dead

To know you not religion
That is His desire
Lover of your soul
A heart that burns with fire

Find out what pleases me
No matter what the cost
I'll hold you oh so close
My lamb no more the lost

Lay down religion
Come dance with your
   King
Don't live by man's rules
I am the song you'll sing

He wants to know you
   child
A Groom who's found His
   Bride
Relationship that's sacred
Walking side by side

Churches have their
   purpose
Yet you're the house He
   seeks
A temple for His glory
Reaching mountain peaks

March 2007

And a woman was there who had been subject to bleeding for twelve years, but no one could heal her. She came up behind him and touched the edge of his cloak, and immediately her bleeding stopped.

—Luke 8:43-44

HIS TOUCH

Twelve years of bleeding
Not finding a cure
One woman's misfortune
A life so unsure

She hears of the Master
The healing of His touch
Her heart overwhelmed
His power could mean so
  much

No one comes near
Years without one friend
One look into His eyes
Could bring this to an end

She presses through the
  crowd
Falling, crawling now
Reaching for His robe
Can I? Could He? But how?

Her fingers reach His
  garment
As power leaves the Son
Her bleeding ends that
  moment
This woman's battle won!

He turns to ask, "Who
  touched Me?"
She falls there at His feet
"Twas I my Lord, for
  healing
I thought we'd never meet"

Your faith has healed you,
  Daughter
Now live your life in peace
Your heart is what I'm after
My touch will never cease!

I've listened to her story
I've read it many times
My life must touch the
  Master
To heal my sinful crimes

She was then and I am now
We both must touch the
  One
That changes lives forever
  more
And mends the heart
  undone

June 2007

'Martha, Martha,' the Lord answered, "you are worried and upset about many things, but only one thing is needed. Mary has chosen what is better, and it will not be taken away from her."

—Luke 10:41-42

WOMAN BE STILL

Woman be still
Sit here at my feet
Stop rushing about
Slow down take a seat

You hustle and bustle
You run here and there
Can't all that wait?
Why do you care?

For things that won't matter
When all's said and done
Be anxious for nothing
The battle's been won

Forget all your stuff
Sit down with your King
Stop all earthly striving
I'll dance while you sing

As I sit here and wait
For your time to be free
I tire of watching
You scurry by me

Your life is a breath
Do you get that dear one?
How much will you give
  me
With each rising sun?

Don't make me a husband
Who's told "Not right now"
Ignoring My longing
Stop running and bow

I weary of waiting
For My bride to sit still
A Mary I'm wanting
A heart toward My will

I'll wait a bit longer
You might lay that aside
For this King and His riches
Will you learn to abide?

July 2007

Printed in the United States
116793LV00001B/61-108/P